SO WHERE ARE WE?

LAWRENCE JOSEPH

FARRAR STRAUS GIROUX

Farrar, Straus and Giroux
18 West 18th Street, New York 10011

Printed in the United States of America
First edition, 2017

Library of Congress Cataloging-in-Publication Data
Names: Joseph, Lawrence, 1948– author.
Title: So where are we? : poems / Lawrence Joseph.
Description: First edition. | New York : Farrar, Straus and Giroux, 2017.
Identifiers: LCCN 2016052195 | ISBN 9780374266677 (hardcover) |
    ISBN 9780374717186 (e-book)
Subjects: BISAC: POETRY / American / General.
Classification: LCC PS3560.O775 A6 2017 | DDC 811/.54—dc23
LC record available at https://lccn.loc.gov/2016052195

Designed by Quemadura

Our books may be purchased in bulk for promotional, educational, or
business use. Please contact your local bookseller or the Macmillan
Corporate and Premium Sales Department at 1-800-221-7945, extension
5442, or by e-mail at MacmillanSpecialMarkets@macmillan.com.

www.fsgbooks.com
www.twitter.com/fsgbooks
www.facebook.com/fsgbooks

1 3 5 7 9 10 8 6 4 2

FOR NANCY VAN GOETHEM

Not ignoring what is good, I am quick to perceive a horror, . . . and in the wild conceits that swayed me to my purpose, two and two there floated into my inmost soul.

HERMAN MELVILLE, *Moby-Dick*

CONTENTS

SO WHERE ARE WE?

A FABLE

Great bronze doors of Trinity Church, hours
told by the sounds of bells. A red

tugboat pushes a red and gold barge
into the Narrows. A bench in the shadows

on a pier in the Hudson. The café
on Cornelia Street, the music,

now whose voice might that be? Diffuse,
invisible, energy. The flow of data

since the attacks has surged.
Technocapital, permanently, digitally,

semioticized, virtually unlimited
in freedom and power, taking

billions of bodies on the planet
with it. Future, past, cosmogonies,

the void, are in whose vision?
Ever-deepening, ravenous

cruelty, viciousness, annihilation,
defended and worshipped.

But is there a more beautiful city—parts
of it, anyway? Another path to the harbor,

the border between sea and land
fluctuating, a line, a curve. Peck Slip

to Water Street to Front Street
to Pine, to Coenties Slip to Pearl

to Stone Street to Exchange Place,
the light in majestic degrees.

This is a fable. A final nail
driven in. The Recording Angel

completes the exactest chronicle.
Blake, with blazing eyes, loves

issues of eternal time. Gauguin
puts a final green on the canvas

of the *Self-Portrait with Yellow
Christ*, to complicate the idea.

SO WHERE ARE WE?

So where were we? The fiery
avalanche headed right at us—falling,

flailing bodies in midair—
the neighborhood under thick gray powder—

on every screen. I don't know
where you are, I don't know what

I'm going to do, I heard a man say;
the man who had spoken was myself.

What year? Which Southwest Asian war?
Smoke from infants' brains

on fire from the phosphorus
hours after they're killed, killers

reveling in the horror. The more obscene
the better. The point at which

a hundred thousand massacred
is just a detail. Asset and credit bubbles

about to burst. Too much consciousness
of too much at once, a tangle of tenses

and parallel thoughts, a series of feelings
overlapping a sudden sensation

felt and known, those chains of small facts
repeated endlessly, in the depths

of silent time. So where are we?
My ear turns, like an animal's. I listen.

Like it or not, a digital you is out there.
Half of that city's buildings aren't there.

Who was there when something was, and a witness
to it? The rich boy general conducts the Pakistani

heroin trade on a satellite phone from his cave.
On the top floor of the Federal Reserve

in an office looking onto Liberty
at the South Tower's onetime space,

the Secretary of the Treasury concedes
they got killed in terms of perceptions.

Ten blocks away the Church of the Transfiguration,
in the back a Byzantine Madonna—

there is a God, a God who fits the drama
in a very particular sense. What you said—

the memory of a memory of a remembered
memory, the color of a memory, violet and black.

The lunar eclipse on the winter solstice,
the moon a red and black and copper hue.

The streets, the harbor, the light, the sky.
The blue and cloudless intense and blue morning sky.

IN A POST-BUBBLE
CREDIT-COLLAPSE ENVIRONMENT

No clouds, now, nearer to Brooklyn Bridge
than the Bridge is to the Heights. Half a block east,

barefoot on shards of glass, a towel wrapped
around his waist, shaving cream on the left side

of his face—a block south, beside a fire hydrant,
a leg found severed at the knee. Internal or external—

what difference does it make? I shake the snow
from my coat, take off my gloves, set them

on the counter. I step back onto Spring Street,
and, on Greenwich, start downtown. Sight and sound

reconfigured, details, truths, colors, and shapes
round out the aesthetic. Things changed

and unchanged, not just in abstract ways.
This young man, yellow pants, undershirt,

stands eating from a garbage bin, patches of ice
on the East River esplanade. One World

Trade Center's structural steel has reached
the fifty-second of a hundred and four stories.

The light in a pink and a coral, moving through
pink and violet scumbled over pink, turning red

on violet. That was yesterday's twilight—this afternoon
white and gray, and hot. Is everything between

six banks and everything else connected, does the old
money ultimately determine the new? "It's really, really

tight out there, how can you *not* think about it?"
is her answer, while seated on the sidewalk at the corner

of Wall and Broad across from the illuminated
Stock Exchange, with backpack and smartphone,

mineral water, sleeping bag, bananas, figs,
police vans parked on Nassau, helicopters

circling overhead, her presence digitally monitored.
In a post-bubble credit-collapse environment

three hundred and fifty percent interest rates on payday loans
and the multi-trillion-dollar market in credit default swaps

are history. "Sub-moron"—the assistant district attorney
bursts into laughter—"drops his coin into the pay phone,

then goes and orders retaliation from the Tombs."
Sunday's forecast, the high tide to coincide

with Irene's heavy rains and hurricane-force winds,
sea level to rise four, five feet at the Battery.

And the puzzles surrounding the cosmological constant,
spacetime imploded into existence. Ten to fifty years
between asbestos breathed and mesothelioma
discovered, a rare form of cancer in the lungs
or heart, or, if in the stomach, spreading
quickly to the liver or spleen. Uploaded
onto one of a half a billion or so blogs: "The human
imagination? A relatively paltry thing, a subproduct,
merely, of the neural activity of a species
of terrestrial primate"; and in another, that other
dimension, the Hudson River, black and still,
the day about to open at the Narrows' edge.
Light on a mountain ash bough, a fresh chill's
blue sensation in the eyes. One week buds, then
the temperature's up and the landscape turns yellow,
in a few days the wind scratches the blossoms,
in a few weeks the sun scorches the leaves.

I, too, see God adumbrations, I, too, write
a book on love. Who, here, appears, to touch the skin.

Hundreds of thousands of square miles of lost Arctic sea ice, bits of bone on killing grounds, electromagnetic air. Atrocious and bottomless states of mind, natural as air.

And when, then, the imagination is transmogrified
into circles of hatred, circles of vengeance
and killing, stealing and deceit? Behind
the global imperia is the interrogation cell. It's not
a good story. Neither the Red Crescent
nor journalists are permitted entry, the women tell
how men and boys are separated, taken in buses
and never seen again, tanks in the streets
with machine guns with no shells in the barrels
because the army fears that those who will use them
might defect. Who knows what has happened,
what is happening, what will happen? God knows.
God knows everything. *The* boy? He is much more
than Mafia; he, and his, own the country. His militias
will fight to the death if for no other reason than
if he's overthrown they will be killed, too. "Iraq,
you remember Iraq, don't you?" she shouts,
a refugee. Her English is good. Reached via Skype,
she speaks anonymously, afraid of repercussions.
"You won't believe what I have seen"—her voice

lowered, almost a whisper—"a decapitated
body with a dog's head sewn on, for example."
Yes, I know, it's much more complicated than that.
"It's the arena right now where the major players are,"
the Chairman of the Joint Chiefs concludes
his exclusive CNN interview. Dagestan—its province
in the North Caucasus—is what the Russians compare
it to, warring clans, sects; Lebanese-like civil war
will break out and spread across the region. Online,
a report—Beirut, the Associated Press—
this morning, "28 minutes ago. 4 Said to Be Dead
at Syrian University," one, Samer Qawass,
thrown, it's said, by pro-regime students
out of the fifth floor window of his dormitory room,
dying instantly from the fall.

Its geography similar to Istanbul's—
read for Lake Huron, the Black Sea,
for the St. Clair River, the Bosporus,
for Lake St. Clair, the Sea of Marmara,
for the Detroit River, the Dardanelles,
and for Lake Erie, the Mediterranean—
a natural place for Ford and Olds to open factories,
strategically near the Pittsburgh steel mills, Akron
rubber plants, Mesabi iron ore range.
Here, in ultimate concentration, is industrial
America—Chrysler, Continental, Budd, Hudson,
in an area not much larger than two square miles,
ninety to a hundred thousand employed on two
or three shifts—the capital of a new planet, the one
on wheels. Whacked-out, stamped-out connecting rods,
the steady blown-out flare of furnaces, hammer-die
brought down on anvil-die, oil-holes drilled and oil-
grooves cut—Fordism was Gramsci's word to describe
mass assembly based on systems of specialized
machines operating within organizational domains

of vertically integrated conglomerates fed by small
and medium-sized units coordinated by methods
of marketing exchange—an epical, systemic violence.
Anonymous's eyes pop as he laughs and says
"dragged the old coon from his car, kicked him till
he shit himself, and then we set the auto on fire—God
Jesus was it a show!" How many summers after that
the Motor City burned to the ground? Soon several new
regimes of redistributed wealth would alter the way
capitalism proceeded, a squad of police breaks down
the union hall door, swinging crowbars and tossing canisters
of Mace—around the time the long depression started.
There are stalks of weeds in sunlit snow, an abandoned
house surrounded by acres of snow. The decay apparently
has frightened the smart money away. Metaphorically
underwater—more is owed on properties in Detroit than
they're worth. His hands and feet were bound, found
beaten in a field near Post and Fort, he's in intensive
care at Receiving Hospital, says Sergeant Ollie L. Atkins,
investigators yet to ask him who he is or what happened.
Notice that on the high school baseball diamond is a herd
of goats—attended by whom? Notice, a few doors down,
the stucco-plastered house painted baby blue, walking in front
in a red stocking cap, green specks on his shoes—what
do you think he is thinking? Drive Woodward to Seven Mile,

west on Seven Mile to Hamilton, Hamilton south to the Lodge
Freeway, then the Lodge downtown, and measure the chaos,
drive Mack Avenue east to Seminole, south on Seminole
to Charlevoix, then west on Charlevoix to Van Dyke, south
on Van Dyke to East Jefferson, and remember what isn't.
Ionic pillars carved with grapes and vine leaves no longer
there, deserted houses of gigantic bulk, in which it seems
incredible anyone could ever have lived, no longer there,
Dodge Main's nocturnal gold vapors no longer there,
the constellated bright lights reflected on the Rouge River's
surface no longer there. Narco-capital techno-compressed,
gone viral, spread into a state of tectonic tension and freaky
abstractions—it'll scare the fuck out of you, is what it'll do,
anthropomorphically scaled down by the ferocity of its own
obsolescence. Which of an infinity of reasons explain it?
Which of an infinity of conflagrations implode its destruction?

AN ANCIENT CLARITY OVERLAID

What is thought and felt, believed and dreamed,
reflected on, the plot worked out in constant

depth, what isn't, for the time being, being written
is being worked on—how long will it be,

the one long poem? Tacitus's *Annals*, its half-
Virgilian lines—Kafka's name on a report,

*Risk Classification and Accident Prevention
in Wartime*—expansion of a tendentious language,

an ancient clarity overlaid. What is said
is, objectively, measured by visual and auditory

standards of the street; as of last Wednesday,
it's said, two hundred six thousand,

six hundred three dead, estimated eighteen million
displaced. How will it end—it won't. Vast open-air,

mud-soaked camps, toxic water—no one can say
cluster bombs aren't real. What of my grandparents'

families in Lebanon, in Syria, what of my grandfather,
dead for all but four years of my life, yet

I think of him and talk to him in the present tense.
The beauty of—a scene seen in streetlight.

Rain stopped, she takes my arm, wind icy, gusting,
on Peck Slip, sky streaked velvet. The power of beauty

the proof accorded—so much of her beauty alive in me
to keep me going the time it takes to finish.

Nuance, I know nuance—in her eyes; having
been, will ever be, love in the play of the eyes.

ON UTOPIA PARKWAY

Between Grand Central Parkway and Little Bay,
from One Hundred Sixty-ninth and Hillside

to Union Turnpike—countless days the streets
I take to work. The front yard of roses—

did I write their names down correctly?—
Zephirine, Charis, Proud Land, Drouhin, Blale.

Q-31 bus, among the words I hear are
Jamie, Jamie does not like to be humiliated,

Jamie is not about to forget it, either. Not
physically well, a poor man, arrested

on suspicion of selling cigarettes loose,
on the street, held, choked, left unconscious,

still handcuffed, no cardiopulmonary resuscitation
administered, pronounced dead, the cause of death,

according to the autopsy report, a homicide—
rectally infused puree of hummus, nuts, and raisins,

by employees of the Agency's contractor,
isn't torture, Director of Central Intelligence

explains, but, merely, legally justified means
of enhanced interrogation. 3708 Utopia Parkway

was Joseph Cornell's small wooden frame house.
He might have worked on the *Medici Slot Machine*

on his kitchen table, a Renaissance Box, a theater
he called it, the Medici and Mussolini's Fascist state

set in metaphorical relation, its inner lines
the lines of the floor plan of the Pitti Palace

the inclusion of an actual compass rose the expression
of an ascent from the temporal to the spiritual.

In what place, the Federal Reserve's
monetary spigots and banks' access

to cash pieced together with indexed futures, to reduce
the market's decline—in what places, violations

of which forms of which eternal laws?
Is it error, the idea that no place, too, is a place?

On the corner of Utopia Parkway and Union Turnpike,
in red-blue twilight abstracted into an energy

blowing it apart, in spaces of language transformed
and coded, to be decoded and recoded in the future.

I will have writings written all over it
    in human words: wrote Blake. A running
form, Pound's Blake: shouting, whirling
    his arms, his eyes rolling, whirling like flaming
cartwheels. Put it this way, in this language:
    a blow in the small of the back from a rifle butt,
the crack of a blackjack on a skull, face
    beaten to a pulp, punched in the nose
with a fist, glasses flying off, "fuckin' Wobblie
    wop, hit him again for me," rifle barrel slammed
against the knees, so much blood in the eyes,
    rain, and the night, and the shooting pain
all up and down the spine, can't see. Put it
    this way: in the sense of smell is an acrid
odor of scorched metal, in the sense of sound,
    the roaring of blowtorches. Put it in this
language: labor's value is abstract value,
    abstracted into space in which a milling machine
cutter cuts through the hand, the end of her thumb

nearly sliced off, metal shavings driven in, rapidly
infected. Put it at this point, the point at which
    capital is most inhumane, unsentimental,
out of control: the quantity of human labor in
    the digital manufacture of a product is progressing
toward the economic value of zero, the maintenance
    and monitoring of new cybernetic processes
occupied by fungible, commodified, labor
    in a form of indentured servitude. Static model,
dynamic model, alternate contract environments,
    enterprise size and labor market functions,
equilibrium characterization, elasticity of response
    to productivity shocks: the question in this Third
Industrial Revolution is who owns and controls
    the data. That's what we're looking at, labor cheap,
replaceable, self-replicating, marginal, contracted out
    into smaller and smaller units. Them? Hordes
of them, of depleted economic, social value,
    who don't count, in any situation, in anyone's eyes,
and won't count, ever, no matter what, the truth that,
    sooner than later, one way or another, they will simply
die off. In Hanover Square, a freezing dawn,
    inside bronze doors the watchman sips bourbon
and black coffee from a paper cup, sees a drunk or drugged

hedge fund boy step over a passed-out body. Logic
of exploitation. Logic of submission; alienation.
  Eyes fixed on mediated screens, in semiotic
labor flow: how many generations between
    the age of slavery of these States and ours?
Makers we, of perfectly contemplated machines.

WHO TALKS LIKE THAT?

The Narrows are strips of yellow and jade,
Verrazano Bridge silver, horizontal lines

here; and here, someone alone, afraid, in tears,
sad, sunken eyes, emaciated body; and, here,

the speed of a slap, the strain under the skin;
and this murky and absurdly massive figure

bent double under an unknown burden;
and this bandaged wound, smudged contours,

body and mind breached;
                              and I thought this,

waking early, looking out, the too magnificent
to be described unclouded sky, night still

in the west, the eastern horizon crimson,
melting into blue, light's solid pact being

forged without apotheosis, Governors Island,
series of waves, where the two rivers meet.

Who talks like that? I talk like that. Blinding
point of light in which everything converges

everything is revealed. Dense constellations
of abject suffering, hell-holes, hell-time,

integrated into what's configured. Light
not only looked at, but the light we've

looked with, in common with Byzantine
mosaics, iconic, chromatic, glowing, as if

caught by the sunlit sky, revised, added to, a separate
palette kept for each poem, in the present a presence,

here, a man who watches the woman he loves
walking toward him, in Battery Park, in patches

of light, in the birch leaf green, the harbor
bright blue, in pockets of deep green shade.

IN THAT CITY, IN THOSE CIRCLES

In that time, in that place, a few cars, a bus, on Belle Isle
seen from this side of the river, dark blue icy river,
on the other side of the Belle Isle Bridge Uniroyal Tire's
bright silver smoke blown over the river to Canada,
time-bound, space-bound, a distinctive industrial space,
Ford Motor Company Dumping Station, the O-So Soda Pop
warehouse, Peerless Cement, railroad tracks on
the bridge to Zug Island—the smell from Wayne
Soap enough to make you puke—Ideal Bar, icon,
Black Madonna, blood-red slash down her right cheek,
Pulaski, Copeland, Home, Melville streets, City of Detroit
Wastewater Treatment Plant, two large sludge ponds,
two slaughterhouses, one for pigs, one cows. And the empire
news, all ratcheted up, unprecedented the rise in energy prices,
armed forces placed on nuclear alert, plans made
to occupy regions of Kuwait, Saudi Arabia, and Abu Dhabi,
surpluses deposited in New York banks, so-called petro-dollars
recycled in high-interest loans to Mexico, Brazil, Argentina—
and, not too long after that really, millions of barrels a day
cut off again, British Petroleum declaring force majeure,

major contracts canceled, the Rotterdam spot market
soaring, the second oil shock fully under way, Arc of Crisis,
the State Department's name of the policy implemented
to spread tribal and religious instability in the Near East
and Soviet Union's southern republics. Intrinsically
curved, the gravitational field, S-curved lines; glue
sprayed, vinyl top stretched and trimmed into place,
lead solder set in the crack between roof and body;
fury of truth, its enigmas, its blinding illuminations marked
in the margin of Hayden's *American Journal*—Hayden's
Cosmic Ouija, the mathematics of the message. Like that,
the music, sweet and funky, Detroit music, backbeat
and beat, tempos extreme, churchy sometimes, rhymes
at ends of and inside the lines, the music made is made
for love, asleep in each other's arms—where, there, we are,
and nothing else matters—there, where the sidewalk heaves,
strapped by weeds, front door boarded by two-by-fours,
an address only a 5, the other numbers missing; and the red dog
sniffing the rusted motor, picking up a scent; "and these
Maronite warlords," he says—here from Lebanon,
my Armenian friend, long, late lunch, Grecian Gardens,
grilled lamb chops, green beans, roasted potatoes, a bottle
of Tsantali Rapsani—"they're trying to force a tax on us
in East Beirut, to finance their militias"—and Niggers Suck,
a sign, on the Southampton Street side of Finney High

the White Hoods hang out on, Black Killers, Errol Flynns
surrounded, switchblades then gunshots, police in riot gear,
media coverage, front-page headlines, *Free Press* and *News*—
and the incarcerated, burned with cattle prods, hit and hit again
with blackjacks at the Second Precinct station—in this air,
raw, still, twelve years ago, the twenty-fourth of July,
General Throckmorton's five thousand paratroopers,
recently returned from Vietnam, authorized
under the Insurrection Act of eighteen-seven, M16s, M79
grenade launchers, lines of deployment set up direct
to the Pentagon, a state of war declared—in that time,
in that city, in those circles; facts of feeling; to call out fact.

WATER STREET

Nothing between us and Brooklyn Bridge
seen from our windows—on the other side of Pearl,

Dover is Frankfort, along the Bridge toward
City Hall—Governors, Staten, Liberty islands,

the harbor, violet and gray, a passing barge
piled with sand, ebony, the East River, the Heights

gold, rain pouring down, massed angles washed
by spacious light, air cleared, an amber luster,

thick, bristling shore of cranes on platforms,
gulls appearing, gleaming white flakes, Manhattan

Bridge, farther up the shore, brushed green.
Images, afterimages, in aftertime, remembered

time, in love's optic, love's characters; in sounds,
in shapes and colors, the same things thought, the thing

said is said in words refracted, pressed in the mind,
among them, now, my peers, vicious and cyanotic,

in the inmost wheels of the machinery of state,
in the invisible axle of the state, radar-jamming F-4G

Wild Weasel missiles, bursts of fire, magenta-tinged
halos circling Baghdad, Operation Desert Storm.

In remembered time, the moon is red, and patches
of red cloud; a finger drawn around the rim

of a cognac snifter; at the sight of a child
with enormous protuberant eyes squeezing

handkerchiefs in both fists, my own anger vanished.
Along these lines, the trouble I'm having

comprehending the schizophrenic prisoner
on death row must be forced to take antipsychotic

medication to make him sane enough to execute,
the drugs, according to the prosecution, beneficial

to him, his eligibility for execution the only unwanted
consequence. And, again, that self that lay hidden,

who speaks in a whisper; and ongoing revelations
in series of circles. Or, say, Water Street,

South Street Seaport, seated outdoors, late June,
early evening, strips of bright silver-pink clouds,

trio of bass, keys, drums; or, let's say,
Water Street, Bridge Café, that February

gray winter day, table in the back, near
the window, up along Dover the Bridge.

And when we're evacuated—mind snapped and snapping
snapped back—in the fundament of things. What you said,
explosions so fierce you feared your eardrums punctured,
the building shook, it moved so much you thought it would crash,
I was, you said, thinking of you so much, you hoped, you said,
not too many were dead, afraid that if this is war
a chemical-warfare agent is in the air, you couldn't see a thing,
heavy, mud-colored, swirling, brown, black, gray,
fine dust particles, it looked like a solid curtain of nightmare,
you said, and, you said, you were frightened. And tower fragments
the size of football fields falling in every direction, seawater
pumped from the Hudson through hoses attached to fire trucks
near West Street, and at night, candles lit at windows
to let the others know they're not alone. Small park
across Queens Boulevard, the leafless oak against the dark
green dusk air, strips of shadow along the pavement's edge.
Twenty-seventh Sunday in Ordinary Time—"And how long,
my God, have I cried out the violence to you, but you do not
intervene, how long have I cried out for help, my God,
but you do not listen"—from the Book of the Prophet Habakkuk.

Today, sunny and windy, blustery tonight and cold.
"Marines and Army May Scour Caves, U.S. General Says,"
headline in the *Times*. No longer in the government,
but on the inside with those in the government, the Taliban
in Afghanistan won't last another month, he says, Sudan
or, maybe, next the Bekáa Valley, but Iraq, there's no evidence
Iraq was involved, but we feel it is, we feel it, he says,
and anyway, he smiles, conditions are, now, ideal to take it.
Acid mist, volatile organic compounds, dangerous levels
of asbestos; rising and spiraling white steam;
blowtorch-produced green vapor, pit fumes,
white, stinking, transformed in pink light until clouds
of smoke obscure it. A common fate pain can't forget;
incessantly pulled apart; in this memory's light.

IN PARENTHESES

I

As I said, I'm a lawyer. Technically speaking,
is a head blown to pieces by a smart bomb a beheading?

II

Infinitely compressible, yet expandable, time,
and curved space, in the preface to Lucretius's
first book of *De Rerum Natura* is a tribute to Venus,
in the last book a description of the plague.

III

Estimated one to two thousand militia, gangs,
really, of fifteen to three thousand
armed killers, in separate, overlapping
networks, difficult to differentiate, and now this,
to quote an anonymous State Department source,
what no one could have predicted,
this phenomenon's, the caliphate's, rise,

nothing since the triumph
of the Vandals in Roman North Africa
this sudden, this incomprehensible.

IV

In the technocapital sphere
absolute principles of profit growth,
of value accumulation, the absolute freedom
to recombine the production of raw materials
into virtual information
in spaces of time, info-time.

V

A theological-political fragment,
a mythographical, scriptural, text,
and sorrow, to understand the meaning
of sorrow, Saint Sorrow,
the addressee of my avowal,
Saint Sorrow's stern vigil necessary to keep.

V I

Hyperviolence is the word, of epic proportions,
a species thing, the point at which
violence becomes ontology,
these endless ambitious experiments in destruction,
a species grief.

V I I

Quite often, almost daily,
in fact, I have strong impressions of eternity,
my ancestors are there, too,
in the shadows—my mother, my father,
grandmothers, grandfathers, whom I refuse
to let perish—whispering to me to be careful.

V I I I

What's that about? Someone I heard say
that to say that Hispanics are East Asian
is sort of like saying that Arabs are white.

IX

Hear that, that man's face being stepped on,
skull being cracked by the baton stick, head
slammed against the concrete edge, blood
in his eyes, body limp, in the process now
of being handcuffed.

X

I am speaking of a law, now, understand,
that point at which bodies locked in cages
become ontology, the point at which
structures of cruelty, force, war,
become ontology. The analog
is what I believe in, the reconstruction
of the phenomenology of perception
not according to a machine,
more, now, for the imagination to affix to
than ever before.

IN THIS LANGUAGE,
IN WAR'S REVOLUTIONS

In this language, in war's revolutions, voice
in the U-2 spy plane, in the stratosphere;

and, here, pilotless Predators firing Hellfire
missiles, secret surveillance installation, Langley

Air Force Base, millions of hours of high-altitude
photographs, monitored cell phones, classified

instant-messaging; and radar, laser, infrared sensor
information systems, artificial-intelligence-interpreted

drones enabled to carry out analysis in flight,
autonomous weapons, targets selected,

engaged without human intervention, no costly
or difficult to obtain raw materials

required to mass-produce, in a matter of time
bought and sold on the black market. Or,

in the city Baghdad, named Sutis by its founder,
Nebuchadnezzar, here where the prophet Daniel

propounded his dream, a grenade is slipped
in the pocket of each victim, wire linked

to a battery, detonator pressed, bodies blown apart,
the execution party walks away laughing

in clouds of smoke and dust. His family, old money—
a bank, hotels, steel manufacturing, pharmaceuticals—

but listen, he says, this is a country owned
ninety-five percent by a clique, so you do business

with them, then I see him on television,
Nebuchadnezzar, his hair being searched for lice,

patting his cheek as if to identify an aching tooth. Syria,
once the greatest of lands, wrote Pliny;

with its different divisions and names:
the part that borders on Arabia, Palaestina;

and Phoenicia, on the coast of the Phoenician Sea;
and, in its interior, Damascena; and, to the south,

Babylonia; and, between the Tigris and Euphrates,
Mesopotamia; and the parts beyond Mount Taurus,

Sophene and Armenia Adiabene—call it
Syria, geopolitical interests mapped out, reconfigured—

is it proto-world-war now playing out?—
the law of nature playing out is simply

to kill. This killing, in this video, is aestheticized:
pilot, alive, alternated with bodies burned

in strikes, lit powder fuse set to clothes
drenched in gasoline, camera angle close,

terror on the faces gone viral. Look, this is
off the record, Chief of Staff, Air Force,

after his briefing on combined, strategic, international
aerial bombardment, is said to have said,

to truly slow them down you have to take
Ramadi, Mosul, Falluja, Tel Afar, Raqqa.

MADE OF THIS, SENSORY FACT

And in this space,
in its own laws—

time in inmost
memory, mind

drifts—here
rain, here,

in the White Columns doorway—
and, thin, the moon,

a reflection on the harbor's
velvet darkness,

red barge lights—fireflies
in Madison Square Park, hot,

bilgy July night—long
noonday walk, Villa Borghese

gardens into Via Veneto,
Piazza Barberini,

Tritone fountain—Bernini's
Triton God

as if raised
from the sea—

twilight, Brooklyn Bridge,
blacks and golds

ascendant, April's
iridescent blue, purple

ground, mauve sky.
                              In

the present,
sounds in the heart

I lose my way in—
there, in a sea

of wishes, there,
sounds of whispering

snow.
      But I

thinking
      of these things,

in the sidereal
realm of these things,

this part of me
in certain

eternities—I believe that.
Brooding-sight,

made of this,
sensory fact,

what hits it aslant,
upon the long axis

of the most
intimate concern to us,

aggregated
horrors accomplished

cause no diminution
of splendor,

                one
and one

in the inmost heart,
consciousness-mirrored,

solidified
in almost solid light. And so

the sun
itself has survived, nothing more,

they,
having fucked,

light
with love,

heavy with sleep,
in the first black

light of dream, one, two
light seconds away.

OF WHAT WE KNOW NOW

And that February cloudless night, deep, now, in its
own reflection, golden full moon's dark blue penumbra;
and ice sheets collapsing causing earthquakes, rattling
seismographs thousands of miles away, mountain-fire
smoke, wind-driven out to sea, enveloping offshore
oil platforms. Violent, narco-state-administered opium
in transit, biomass of manufactured plastics resistant
to decay weighing more than billions of humans
the violence along social fracture-lines, anarcho-capital
circulating at infinite speed, returning to itself even
before taking leave of itself, on its own plane of intelligence,
warping, dissolving nature—the poem in its voracities
of contemplation—the poem's judgment proven, exact—
thought to thought, configurations, in fifty years these words
will be written fifty years ago, that is, now. Spectacles—ugly:
metal molds stuffed with ammonium nitrate, gasoline,
chunks of steel shredded into hot shrapnel on impact,
barrel bombs. Of what we know now, algo-trading in multiple
    venues,

a third of it run by phantom liquidity providers, turbocharged
    scalpers;
evidence, irrefutable, in the Commission on Stratigraphy's
Official Report, the Anthropocene (human-driven geological
epoch, never seen before stoichiometric ratios, industrial
metals—cadmium, chromium, nickel, copper, mercury, lead,
zinc—widely and rapidly dispersed into air, earth, water)
beginning around the time I was born; the failure
to apprehend the countless participants in the countless
mass killings, an issue the Mechanism for International
Criminal Tribunals has not, as of yet, effectively addressed.

IN ONE DAY'S ANNALS

Inscrutable the Muse Who Selects My Fate;
Breaking News Graphic, Word of the Attack

Spreads; History of the Great Exegesis;
The Gospel According to Saint Matthew;

Truly Stupendous Levels of Hatred;
and others, too many to mention, each

with their own characters, dialogues, scenes.
In his eternity, up to his waist in a pool

of green liquid poisons, the president who
raises his eyebrows, blows out his cheeks,

purses his lips, feigns surprise, smirks.
In one day's annals, seen through Sweet

Revenge's windows, Carmine Street's
gold dusk light, purplish bronze shielding

Teardrop Park turning a misty gray, slipping
on the ice, falling, headfirst, onto Rector Street,

Number Two subway train's lights go out—
he continues to play—lights on again—

he finishes, lifts his guitar and kisses it—
on one of fifteen years of Wednesdays,

millions of gallons of untreated sewage
discharged from the North River Wastewater

Treatment Plant's pipes into the Hudson
and Harlem rivers. What's clear,

delicate, beautiful, what's ugly, horrifying;
but why we go to the end of the night

is for no other reason than another
moral to the story, the primal paradise

the body remembers, elemental stasis
of infinities of light and time, hypostatic.

ON PERIPHERIES OF THE IMPERIUM

I

Eye of the hurricane the Battery, the Hudson
breached, millions of gallons of it
north on West Street filling Brooklyn-Battery
Tunnel, overflowing into the World Trade Center site,
East River, six-to-eight-foot wall of water on South,
Front, Water, John, Fulton, Pearl,
Brooklyn Bridge's woven cables lifted delicately
in hurricane sky.

II

Perhaps I make too much of it, that time,
Eldon Axle, brake plates dipped
in some sort of liquid to protect them from
dust, dirt, metal chips the grinding caused—
that time, night shift, press-machine shop
on Outer Drive, rolls of stainless steel put in,
fixed up, because the work you do is around fire
your cuticles burn if the mask's not on right.

III

When the mind is clear, to hear the sound
of a voice, of voices, shifts in the attitude
of syllables pronounced. When the mind
is clear, to see a Sunday, in August, Shrine
of Our Lady of Consolation, Carey, Ohio,
at a holy water font, a mother washes
her six-year-old's fingers crushed in an accident
so that they'll heal.

I V

So what percentage of Weasel Boy's DNA
do you think is pure weasel? Tooth-twisted,
Yeats's weasels, in "Nineteen Hundred
and Nineteen," fighting in a hole.

V

Conflated, the finance vectors, opaque
cyber-surveillance, supranational cartels,
in the corporate state's political-economic singularity
the greatest number of children
in United States history are, now, incarcerated,
having been sentenced by law.

VI

A comic dimension to it, on this F-Train
to One Hundred Sixty-ninth Street
in Queens? He doesn't want to disturb you,
but, see, he was stabbed in the face
with an ice pick, he lost his left eye—
lid pried open with thumb and forefinger—
here, look, he'll show you—
a white-and-pink-colored iris.

Fulton near Pearl, dug up to lay the new Fulton Center
subway power lines, a stone wall, three feet high,
in silt-muck seven feet below street level, inside it
a ceramic bird's half-blue, half-yellow head, stem
of a pipe, chunk of glazed seventeenth-century stoneware
decorated with the arms of Amsterdam, huge turkey
vultures taking a liking to the landfill, the preferred source
of food for peregrine falcons is pigeons. His own police
department, the mayor brags, seventh largest army
in the world, and remember, too, the United Nations
is here, so he has his own state department, too, an entrée
into the diplomatic world. Gets deep inside the head, this man
says—he's permanently disabled—affects you emotionally,
what's happened here, pulverized glass, concrete, lead,
asbestos traces, crap, he calls it, here, he shows you
the albuterol and epinephrine he must at all times carry.
To cool your head you walk. Statue of Confucius on
the Bowery, rice-bean cakes, chicken feet, curried squid
on Division, under the Manhattan Bridge, on Canal to Seward
Park, a piece of torn yellow tape tied to a tree, this woman

shouting into her smartphone go fuck yourself and die,
large black letters—in Russian?—on the freighter's hull
fade imperceptibly into one another. Supply route to deliver
food to non-government-held areas in Aleppo severed,
three hundred thousand at risk of starvation, electricity
cut off, markets, houses, schools, bombed hospitals,
migrant smuggling worth more, now, than the trade in drugs
and weapons—profits confined to those in a position
to play, venture capital, private equity, hedge-fund operators,
stock buybacks leveraged, paid for by money borrowed
at artificially low Federal Reserve Bank-charged interest rates,
newly minted Treasury obligations validating private-sector
asset prices into the trillions, statist-sanctioned racketeering—
is what it is. "But after all, I'm a lawyer. So I can never get
away from evil," Kafka said—Franz Kafka, legal officer,
Workers' Accident Insurance Institute, the Kingdom
of Bohemia—whose report *Measures for Preventing
Accidents from Wood-Planing Machines*, among other things,
depicts work-related dissevered fingers. Flint is what it is.
Knowingly to force the poor to purchase and use toxic water
isn't a form of chemical warfare, isn't a form of genocide?

Revelations reoccurring, he who is babbling away
in James Madison Plaza, in what goes around,
what comes around, light made holy by the fury
of the tears with which it mingles, simple enough,
when looked at directly, the child, shy and fearful,
who won't speak. And for the record, the mind,
like the night, has a thousand eyes—
sparrows in the bushes; a small cat
rolls in the snow; sleet pounding the windows.
In the space of a memory, the facade of a church,
an angel on each side of a fiery wheel.

BACK TO THAT

I

Spread on the station's concrete floor,
backpack with files of papers,

water bottles,
a large plastic bag filled with blankets,

spittle dripping from his lips.
Up the stairs to Hillside Avenue,

I look for the Q-30 or Q-31 bus,
signs in Urdu across the street.

II

And this, now, nuclear
modernization, new

nuclear ordnance and delivery
systems, stealth-missile-firing

submarines, long-range
bombers, steerable

bombs, unprecedented
precision, flexibility,

cost
one, two

trillion,
to be completed by the hundredth anniversary

of the atomic bombs
unleashed on

Hiroshima,
Nagasaki.

III

The poem of what is touched
incandescently, the poem
measuring out its own circle—lucky poet,
no rules to adhere to,
except never to make an aesthetic mistake.

IV

And in yet another space,
Pasolini's poem

"A un Papa," written
after Pacelli's, Pius XII's, death,

the real evil is not to do good,
wrote Pasolini;

what Pacelli might have done
but did not do—

no greater sinner than Pacelli,
wrote Pasolini.

V

What we felt—
something taken from us
we'll never get back—disarticulated,
no language for it, inwardly unstrung.

Our God, wrote Bonnard,
is light—lucent

greens, bronze-gold
in the river's

silver blaze, pink-black-tinged clouds
dissolving,

darkened purple air.
And to mystery rightly reasoned

a logic consigned,
an intimist's mood,

in our transworld now,
our eyes tell us what

we're doing—
we know exactly

what
we're doing—

in what voice
but a comic voice can the voice

of love
truthfully be?

VII

What's going on—
a combination

"Red River Shore,"
"Soon After Midnight,"

song-vibe
is what is going on this

black-gold
October sunset;

you can say what you like
to that.

WHAT MORE IS THERE TO SAY?

December mild, deep January cold,
sunlight filtered through blue haze,

yellow the grass closely pressed,
patches of dirt, in red-and-lavender

twilight, a tugboat in the harbor
clearing the ice. In those circles

in which all heaven breaks loose,
touched by who she is, by what

she wills; in the envisioned heart
inmost issues take the form

of a credo. The God to whom
an account must be rendered,

my dead to whom I pray,
as I, in turn, pray the life once theirs

is transfigured. What a story
to tell, violence from the terror felt,

violence in the suffering, violence
in the mind, collectively modified,

escalated to maximum speed.
So what more is there to say? Many times

the mass of the sun, solar masses
spiraling into spacetime, radiating

energy in gravitational waves, the edges
of the islands soft in the black-gray sky,

on this side of the Battery, near the ferry,
a small bird's footprints, here, in the snow.

New moon, mauve cloud, sea level
higher than normal, the harbor again,

green and gray, punctuated by waves
lashing about. Thickening, the mists,

this early morning; repeated, sounds
of foghorns we hear from afar.

ACKNOWLEDGMENTS

Grateful acknowledgment is made to the editors of the following publications, in which these poems, sometimes in earlier versions, first appeared:

The Common: "In One Day's Annals," "In That City, in Those Circles"

Commonweal: "And for the Record," "On Nature," "That September and October," "In Parentheses"

Freeman's: "What More Is There to Say?"

Granta: "So Where Are We?"

The Kenyon Review: "In This Language, in War's Revolutions," "Of What We Know Now"

London Review of Books: "Here in a State of Tectonic Tension," "Visions of Labor"

The Nation: "Syria," "Who Talks Like That?"

The New Yorker: "A Fable," "In a Post-Bubble Credit-Collapse Environment"

The New York Review of Books: "An Ancient Clarity Overlaid"

The Paris Review: "Is What It Is"

Poetry: "On Utopia Parkway," "On Peripheries of the Imperium"

Subtropics: "Made of This, Sensory Fact," "Back to That"

"Water Street" appeared in the Academy of American Poets Poem-a-Day Digital Poetry Series.

"So Where Are We?" also appeared in *The Best American Poetry 2012* (ed. Mark Doty) and *The Best of the Best American Poetry: 25th Anniversary Edition* (ed. Robert Pinsky); "Syria," in *The Best American Poetry 2013* (ed. Denise Duhamel); and "Visions of Labor," in *The Best American Poetry 2016* (ed. Edward Hirsch; Scribner Poetry).

"So Where Are We?" is included in *Tales of Two Cities: The Best & Worst of Times in Today's New York* (ed. John Freeman; Penguin Books, 2015), and "Here in a State of Tectonic Tension" in *Tales of Two Americas: Stories of Inequality in a Divided Nation* (ed. John Freeman; Penguin Books, 2017).